To my YesKid:

_____

With love from:

_____

Contents

Christian Media Publishers,
PO Box 4502, Durbanville, 7551
www.christianmediapublishing.com

Author: Ewald van Rensburg

Illustrations, Design & Layout: Lilani Brits

Publishing Project Manager: Noeline N Neumann

Reg No 2010/008573/07

Text: Maranatha Publishing: Used by kind agreement.

Printed in Malaysia through PrettyInPress Productions.

First Editon, second printing, 2013
ISBN 978-1-920460-47-1

CMP-kids books have been developed with your child's
developmental phases and unique temperament in mind.
For a full explanation of the **unique temperament** and **developmental
phases** icons visit the CMP website **www.cmpublishing.co.za**

YesKids
Bible Stories
- about Jesus -

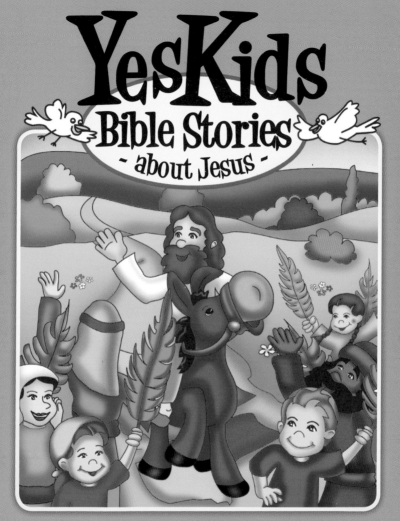

Kids saying YES! For Jesus

Written by Ewald van Rensburg
Illustrations by Lilani Brits

christian media publishing **Kids**
pointing children in the **right direction**

1. Jesus is born

(Luke 1 & 2)

Mary lived in the town of Nazareth.
She was engaged to Joseph.
One day she had a visitor.
This wasn't just anybody; it was one
of God's archangels, Gabriel, who paid
her a visit. He told her that she was
going to have a baby, and this baby
would be the Son of God. "How can
this happen?" Mary asked. "I am not
married yet."

Gabriel told her not to
worry, because
nothing is
impossible with
God. The baby
would be a miracle
sent from heaven.

Mary answered the angel, "Tell God I am willing to obey. He can do anything he wants with me." The angel left, and her life was never the same again. Mary and Joseph were married later. It was the greatest moment when the special baby from heaven was born in Bethlehem and she held him in her arms. Joseph called the baby Jesus. Yes, this baby Jesus would change the whole world.

Come, let's pray together:

Lord, I worship and praise you because nothing is impossible with you. Amen.

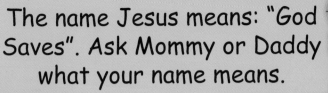

The name Jesus means: "God Saves". Ask Mommy or Daddy what your name means.

7

2. Here comes King Jesus
(Matthew 21)

When they came near to Jerusalem, Jesus said to his friends, "Bring me a young donkey." He told them where to find the donkey and what they had to say to its owner. Jesus' friends went to the place where the donkey was. They were about to take the donkey when the owner asked, "Why are you taking my donkey?"

"Jesus needs him," they replied. When the man heard this, he was satisfied. He gave the donkey to them straight away.

Jesus rode the donkey into the city of Jerusalem. Crowds of people lined the street. They waved palm branches in the air and shouted, "Praise the Lord. Here comes the King!"

Come, let's pray together:

Lord Jesus, I want to sing
your praises everyday.
Amen.

Tell everyone that Jesus is king of your life.

3. The cross

(Matthew 27)

Jesus' enemies wanted to kill him. They went to Pontius Pilate, the most important man in the country.
They told him to find Jesus guilty of a crime; but Pilate could not find anything that Jesus had done wrong.

Pilate decided to ask the people what he should do. When they saw Jesus they all shouted, "Crucify him!"
Jesus' enemies had told them to do this. Pilate told them to crucify Jesus at a place called Golgotha. There they hung Jesus on a cross between two criminals.

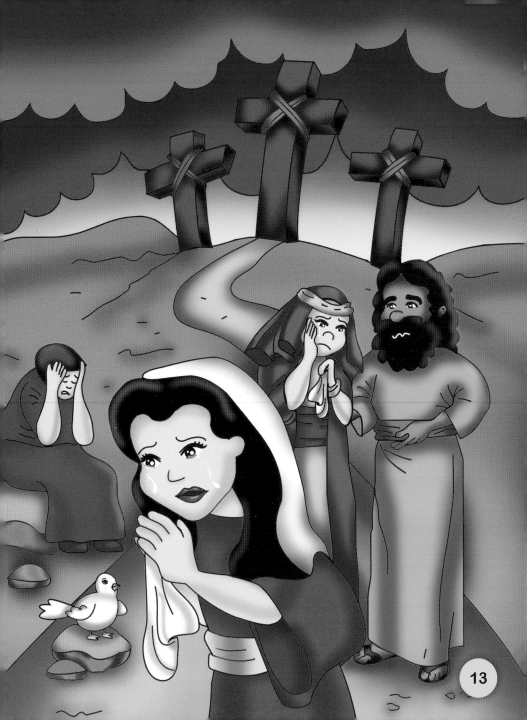

While he was dying on the cross, Jesus asked God to forgive those same people who were being so cruel to him.

Jesus died on a Friday afternoon which is now known as Good Friday, because on that day Jesus made it possible for people to be friends with God once again.

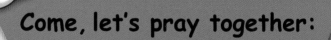

Come, let's pray together:

Lord Jesus, thank you that you died on the cross for my sins.
Amen.

Jesus died on the cross so that all the wrong things we do — our sins — can be forgiven.

15

4. Jesus has risen from the dead! (Matthew 28)

Jesus was buried that Friday in a cave that belonged to his friend Joseph. Everyone was very sad.

Early on the Sunday morning a group of women went to the grave.
They wondered how they would get inside the cave, because a big stone had already been rolled in front of the entrance. But when they got there they found that the stone had already been rolled away . . . and that the grave was empty!

An angel told them that Jesus had risen from the dead.

They were so happy. They rushed back to tell the rest of Jesus' friends the good news. One of the women, Mary Magdalene, went back to the empty grave. "Mary!" she heard someone calling her name. Right away she knew it was Jesus. She ran to tell the others that she had seen Jesus with her own eyes.

Come, let's pray together:

Lord Jesus, thank you that you are alive, and that I will live with you forever. Amen.

Jesus is alive!
And everyone who loves him
will live with him forever,
even when they die.

5. Jesus returns home
(Acts 1)

Jesus' friends were so happy to have him back. They knew that nobody is as powerful as he is. He is even stronger than death.

One day Jesus told them that he had to go back to be with his father in heaven, because heaven is his true home. He also told them not to be sad, because one day they would all join him there!

Jesus and his friends then climbed to the top of a mountain.

A cloud came down and covered them. When the cloud lifted, it took Jesus away. Jesus' friends watched him going to heaven with sad hearts.

Suddenly they saw two angels standing there. The angels said to the disciples (this is the name given to Jesus' special friends) that Jesus would come back one day. They had to go and tell the whole world that Jesus loves everybody.

Come, let's pray together:

Lord Jesus, I know you will return to take me to heaven, because the Bible tells me so. Amen.

Even though Jesus is in heaven, we know he still takes care of us.

Guidelines for parents

Faith Icon

The formation of faith is indeed unique to each child; there are however general characteristics which apply to all children. There are three main ways that children develop faith:

- Parents regularly reading the Bible, telling Bible and other faith based stories, praying together and doing faith building activities with their children (such as the ones found in this book).
- Children ask questions – parents need to take these questions seriously and answer them according to the child's level of understanding.
- Children follow the example of those caring for them.

Emotional intelligence icon

We experience emotions long before we learn the language to be able to express how we are feeling. Therefore it is important that children are taught to verbalise what they are feeling. Use the illustrations accompanying the stories and ask your child how they think the people or animals in the picture feel. This helps them become aware of their own emotions as well as those of others. It provides a learning opportunity where the child can learn appropriate words to express how they are feeling.

Reading icon

A wonderful world opens up for your child when they start learning to read. Enjoy every moment of this exciting adventure with your child. Let them sit on your lap where they can be comfortable and feel safe and secure. Open the book holding it so that you can both see the pages. Read clearly and with enthusiasm. As you know you can read the same story over and over. Point out where you are reading with your finger as you go along. This will help your child to begin to see the relationship between letters, sounds, words and their meaning. Encourage your child's attempts at reading – even of it sounds like gibberish.

Listening skills icon

Listening is an important learning and development skill. You can help develop this skill in your child by encouraging them to listen attentively, and understand what they are hearing. Let them look at the illustrations and then use their imagination to tell the story back to you in their own words. You can also encourage them to do this by asking questions relating to the story. Yet another way is to leave out words from a story the child knows well and let them fill in the missing words.

Vocabulary icon

Use every opportunity to build your child's vocabulary – it is a lifelong gift which you are giving to them. Start with everyday objects and people in the illustrations in books. Point at the picture, say the word, form a short sentence using the word. Repeat it again and then let your child say the word. Try to use the word in another context – if there is a tent in the picture you are looking at then say: we sleep in a tent when we go camping.

Numeracy skills icon

It is important for your child develop numeracy skills. Play simple games such as: "How many ducks are there in the picture? If we add two more ducks how many are there now? Then if three fly away? (use your fingers to illustrate this) How many are left? They also need to recognise the shape of numbers – cut large numbers from cardboard – let your child play with these – place the numbers in order forming a line from one to ten.